Introduction

This is a reprint of an original 12-page narrow pamphlet published in 1929 by the son of the 10th president of the United States, John Tyler.

Lyon Gardiner Tyler was a noted historian, educator and author in his own right — serving as president of William and Mary College for 33 years.

He wrote this pamphlet to help correct the propaganda about the South, and his father, by Northern writers and publishers. It is short, concise and should be read by every student, not only in the South, but in the United States.

It has been reset in a modern typeface with all the original language intact. Also included are some facts about the author, along with his portrait, at the end.

We hope you enjoy our efforts.

— Frank B. Powell, III, Editor

A Confederate Catechism

THE WAR OF 1861-1865

(Third Edition, November 21, 1929)

By LYON GARDINER TYLER

REPRINTED BY

Wake Forest, NC
www.scuppernongpress.com

A Confederate Catechism
The War of 1861-1865

By Lyon Gardiner Tyler

©2015 The Scuppernong Press

First Printing

The Scuppernong Press
PO Box 1724
Wake Forest, NC 27588
www.scuppernongpress.com

Cover and book design by Frank B. Powell, III

All rights reserved

Printed in the United States of America

No part of this book may be reproduced or transmitted in any form or by any means, electronic or mechanical, including photocopying, recording, or by any information and storage and retrieval system, without written permission from the editor and/or publisher.

International Standard Book Number
  ISBN 978-1-942806-03-5

Library of Congress Control Number:
  2015949988

Contents

1. What was the cause of secession in 1861? 1

2. Was slavery the cause of secession or the war? 3

3. Was the extension of slavery the purpose of secession? 3

4. Was Secession the cause of the war? 4

5. What then was the cause of the war? 5

6. Did the South fight for slavery or the extension of slavery? 6

7. Did the South fight for the overthrow of the United States Government? 6

8. What did the South fight for? 8

9. Did the South in firing on Fort Sumter begin the war? 9

10. Why did Lincoln break the truce at Fort Pickens and precipitate the war by sending troops to Fort Sumter? 10

11. Did Lincoln carry on the war for the purpose of freeing the slaves? 12

12. Did Lincoln, by his conquest of the South, save the Union? 13

13. Could Lincoln have "saved" the Union by some other method than war? 14

14. Does any present or future prosperity of the South justify the War of 1861-1865? 16

15. Had the South gained its independence, would it have proved a failure? 16

16. Were the Southerners "rebels" in seceding from the Union? 17

17. Did the South, as alleged by Lincoln in his messages and in his Gettysburg address, fight to destroy popular government throughout the world? 19

18. Was Lincoln's proclamation freeing the slaves worthy of the praise which it has received? 20

19. Would Lincoln have saved the South from the horrors of Reconstruction if he had survived the war? 21

20. Is there any truth in the statement that the South seceded from the Union because it saw itself menaced with the loss of the rule which it had enjoyed from the beginning? 23

About the Author 25

Dedicated to the Truth

1. What was the cause of secession in 1861?

It was the fact that the Union consisted from the first of two jarring nations having different interests, which were brought to the breaking point in 1861 by the intemperate agitation in the North against everything Southern. The breaking point was nearly reached in 1785 when the North sought to stop the development of the South by giving the Mississippi River to Spain, in 1801 when it attempted the immoral act of turning the presidential ticket upside down and making Aaron Burr president, and in 1833 went it imposed upon the South a high protective tariff for the benefit of Northern manufacturers. The breaking point was finally reached in 1861, when after unmitigated abuse of the South, a strictly Northern president was elected by strictly Northern votes upon a platform which repudiated the decision of the Supreme Court of the United States authorizing Southerners to carry their slaves into the territories. This decision gave no material advantage to slavery, as none of the remaining territorial domain was in any way fit for agriculture, but the Southerners resented the attitude of Lincoln and his party as a challenge to their constitutional rights and as a determination on the part of the North to govern the Union thereafter by virtue of a mere numerical majority. The literature of those times shows that such mutual and mortal hatred existed as, in the language of Jefferson, "to render separation preferable to eternal discord." The choice was between remaining in such a Union of hate, or seceding. There was no real peace, and the South seceded because it wanted peace and not strife or war.

2. Was slavery the cause of secession or the war?

No. Slavery existed previous to the Constitution, and the Union was formed in spite of it. Both from the standpoint of the Constitution and sound statesmanship, it was not slavery, but the vindictive, intemperate anti-slavery movement that was at the bottom of all the troubles.

3. Was the extension of slavery the purpose of secession?

No. When South Carolina seceded, she had no certainty that any other Southern state would follow her example. By her act she absolutely shut herself out from the territories and thereby limited rather than extended slavery. The same may be said of the other seceding states who joined her.

4. Was Secession the cause of the war?

No. Secession is a mere civil process having no necessary connection with war. Norway seceded from Sweden, and there was no war. The attempted linking of slavery and secession with war is merely an effort to obscure the issue — "a red herring drawn across the trail." Secession was based (1) upon the natural right of self government, (2) upon the reservation to the States in the Constitution of all powers not expressly granted to the Federal government. Secession was such a power, being expressly excepted in the ratifications of the Constitution by Virginia, Rhode Island and New York. (3) Upon the right of the principal to recall the powers vested in the agent; and upon (4) the inherent nature of all partnerships, which carries with them the right of withdrawal. The States were partners in the Union, and no partnership is irrevocable. The perpetuity spoken of in the Preamble to the Constitution was the expression merely of a *hope* and *wish*. No rights of sovereignty whatever could exist without the right of secession.

5. What then was the cause of the war?

The cause of the war was
(1) the rejection of the right of secession by Lincoln, and
(2) the denial of self government to 8,000,000 people occupying a territory half the size of Europe. Lincoln himself said of these people that they possessed as much moral sense and as much devotion to law and order as "any other civilized and patriotic people." Without consulting Congress, Lincoln sent great armies to the South, and it was the war of a president elected by a minority of the people of

the North. In the World War, Woodrow Wilson declared that "No people must be forced under sovereignty under which it does not choose to live." When in 1903, Panama seceded from Colombia, the United States sided with Panama against Colombia in support of Panama's right to self-government.

6. Did the South fight for slavery or the extension of slavery?

No. For had Lincoln not sent armies to the South, that country would have done no fighting at all.

7. Did the South fight for the overthrow of the United States Government?

No. The South fought to establish its own government. Secession did not destroy the Union, but merely reduced its territorial extent. The United States existed when there were only thirteen states, and it would have existed when there were twenty states left. The charge brought by Lincoln that the aim of the Southerners was to overthrow the government was no more true than if King George III had said that the secession of the American colonies from Great Britain had in view the destruction of the British Government. The government of Great Britain was not destroyed by the success of the American States in 1783. Nor would the government of the United States have been destroyed if the Southern states had succeeded in repelling the attacks of the North in 1861-1865.

8. What did the South fight for?

IT FOUGHT TO REPEL INVASION AND FOR SELF GOVERNMENT, JUST AS THE FATHERS OF THE AMERICAN REVOLUTION HAD DONE. Lincoln himself confessed at first that he had no constitutional right to make war against a state, so he resorted to the subterfuge of calling for troops to suppress "combinations" of persons in the Southern States "too powerful to be suppressed by the ordinary" processes. It is impossible to understand how the Southern States could have proceeded in a more regular and formal manner than they did to show they acted as states and not as mere "combinations." It shows the lack of principle that characterized Lincoln when later he referred to the Southern States as "insurrectionary States."

9. Did the South in firing on Fort Sumter begin the war?

No. Lincoln began the war by secretly attempting to land troops at Fort Pickens in Florida in violation of a truce existing between the Federals and the Confederates at that place. This was long before Fort Sumter was fired on, and Fort Sumter was fired on only after Lincoln had sent an armed squadron to supply and strengthen that Fort. Even supposing that the action of the Confederates in firing on the Fort was unjustifiable, Lincoln was not bound to treat it as a gauge of battle. He knew that all the Confederates wanted was a fort that commanded the Metropolitan city of Charleston — a fort which had been erected for the defense of that city. He knew that they had no desire to engage in a war with the United States. Not every hostile act justifies war, and in the World War this country submitted to having its flag filled full of holes and scores of its citizens destroyed before it went to war. Lincoln, without any violation of his views of government, had an obvious alternative in putting the question of war up to Congress, where it belonged under the Constitution. But he did not do it and assumed the powers of Congress in making laws and enforcing them as an executive. By his mere authority, he enormously increased the Federal army, blockaded Southern ports, and declared Southern privateersmen to be pirates.

10. Why did Lincoln break the truce at Fort Pickens and precipitate the war by sending troops to Fort Sumter?

Lincoln did not think that war would result by sending troops to Fort Pickens, and it would give him the appearance of asserting the national authority. But he knew that hostilities would certainly ensue if he attempted to reinforce Fort Sumter. He was therefore at first in favor of withdrawing the troops from that Fort, and allowed assurances to that effect to be given out by Seward, his Secretary of State. But the deciding factor with him was the tariff question. In three separate interviews, he asked what would become of his revenue if he allowed the government at Montgomery to go on with their ten percent tariff. Final action was taken when nine governors of high tariff states waited upon Lincoln and offered him men and supplies. The protective tariff had almost driven the country to war in 1833; it is not surprising that it brought war in 1861. Indeed, this spirit of spoliation was so apparent from the beginning that at the very first Congress, Grayson, one of our two first Virginia Senators, predicted that the fate reserved to the South was to be "the milk cow of the Union." The *New York Times*, after having on March 21, 1861, declared for separation, took the ground nine days later that the material interest of the North would not allow of an independent South!

11. Did Lincoln carry on the war for the purpose of freeing the slaves?

No. He frequently denied that this was his purpose in waging war. He claimed that he fought the South in order to preserve the Union. Before the war, Lincoln declared himself in favor of enforcement of the fugitive slave act, and he once figured as an attorney to drag back a runaway Negro into slavery. When he became president he professed himself in his inaugural willing to support an amendment guaranteeing slavery in the states where it existed. Wendell

Phillips, the abolitionist, called him a "slave hound."

12. Did Lincoln, by his conquest of the South, save the Union?

No. The old Union was a union based on consent. The present Union is a great Northern nation based on force and controlled by Northern majorities, to which the South, as a conquered province, has had to conform all its policies and ideals. The Federal authority is only Northern authority. Today the Executive, the Cabinet, the Supreme Court, (with one exception), the Ministers at foreign courts are all Northern men. The South has as little share in the government and as little chance of furnishing a president as Norway or Switzerland.

13. Could Lincoln have "saved" the Union by some other method than war?

Yes. If he had given his influence to the resolutions offered in the Senate by John Jay Crittenden, the difficulties in 1861 would have been peaceably settled. These resolutions extended the line of the Missouri Compromise through the territories, but gave nothing to the South, save the abstract right to carry slaves to New Mexico. But most of New Mexico was too barren for agriculture, and not ten slaves had been carried there in ten years. The resolutions received the approval of the Southern Senators and, had they been submitted to the people, would have received their approval both North and South. Slavery in a short time would have met a peaceful and natural death with the development of machinery consequent upon Cyrus H. McCormick's great invention of the reaper. The question in 1861 with the South as to the territories was one of wounded pride rather than any material advantage. It was the intemperate, arrogant and self-righteous attitude of Lincoln and his party that made any peaceable constructive solution of the territorial question impossible. In rejecting the Crittenden resolutions, Lincoln, a minority president, and the Republicans, a minority party, placed themselves on record as virtually preferring the slaughter of 400,000 men of the flower of the land and the sacrifice of billions of dollars of property to a compromise involving a mere abstraction. And they intrigued an unwilling North into the war, and some historians have actually boasted of the trickery.

14. Does any present or future prosperity of the South justify the War of 1861-1865?

No. No present or future prosperity can make a past wrong right, for *the end can never justify the means*. The war was a colossal crime, and the most astounding case of self-stultification on the part of any government recorded in history.

15. Had the South gained its independence, would it have proved a failure?

No. General Grant has said in his *Memoirs* that it would have established "a real and respected nation." The states of the South would have been bound together by fear of the great Northern Republic and by a similarity of economic conditions. They would have had laws suited to their own circumstances, and developed accordingly. They would not have lived under Northern laws and had to conform their policy to them, as they have been compelled to do. A low tariff would have attracted the trade of the world to the South, and its cities would have become great and important centers of commerce. A fear of this prosperity induced Lincoln to make war upon the South. The Southern Confederacy, instead of being a failure, would have been a great outstanding figure in the affairs of the world.

16. Were the Southerners "rebels" in seceding from the Union?

The term "rebel" had no application to the Southern people, however much it applied to the American colonists. The latter called themselves "Patriots" not rebels. Both Southerners in 1861 and Americans in 1776 acted under the authority of their state governments. But while the colonies were mere departments of the British Union, the American States were creators of the Federal Union. The Federal government was the agent of the states for the purposes expressed in the Constitution, and it is absurd to say that the principal can rebel against the agent. President Jackson threatened war with South Carolina in 1833, but admitted that in such an event South Carolinians taken prisoners would not be "rebels" but prisoners of war. The Freesoilers in Kansas and John Brown at Harpers Ferry were undoubtedly "rebels" for they acted without any lawful authority whatever in using force against the Federal Government, and Lincoln and the Republican Party, in approving a platform which sympathized with the Freesoilers and bitterly denounced the Federal Government, were rebels and traitors at heart.

17. Did the South, as alleged by Lincoln in his messages and in his Gettysburg address, fight to destroy popular government throughout the world?

No. This charge was absurd. Had the South succeeded, the United States would still have enjoyed all its liberties, and so would Great Britain, France, Italy, Belgium, Switzerland and all other peoples. The danger to popular government came from Lincoln himself. In conducting the war, Lincoln talked about "democracy" and "the plain people," but adopted the rules of despotism and autocracy, and under the fiction of "war powers" virtually abrogated the Constitution, which he had sworn to support.

18. Was Lincoln's proclamation freeing the slaves worthy of the praise which it has received?

No. His proclamation was a war measure merely. He had no humanitarian purpose in view, and only ten days before its issuance he declared that "the possible consequences of insurrection and massacre in the Southern States" would not deter him from its use, whenever he should deem it necessary for military purposes. (Nicolay and Hay, *Complete Works of Abraham Lincoln, II*, p.235) In his second inaugural message, while professing "malice to none and charity to all," he slandered the South by describing the slave owner as an incarnate demon, who did nothing but lash his slaves, without giving the least requital for their service of 250 years! The Negroes were the most spoiled domestics in the world. The Southerners took the Negro as a barbarian and cannibal, civilized him, supported him, clothed him, and turned him out a devout Christian. Booker T. Washington admitted that the Negro was the beneficiary rather than the victim of slavery.

19. Would Lincoln have saved the South from the horrors of Reconstruction if he had survived the war?

No. Lincoln had shown no kindness to the South while he lived, and there is no reason to suppose that he would have done so had he survived the war. His war violated every law of humanity, and instead of offering pardon to everyone who would submit, as the British General Howe had done in his amnesty proclamation of November 30, 1776, Lincoln in his amnesty proclamation of December 8, 1863, excepted from the benefits of his proclamation everybody in the South of any leading intelligence. It is absurd to ascribe Andrew Johnson's policy of Reconstruction to Lincoln, for Lincoln in his proclamation of July 8, 1864, professed that he was not bound up to any fixed plan whatever. The closest companion of Lincoln and the mastermind of his Cabinet was Edwin M. Stanton, who hated the South and all that concerned it. President Johnson, to his credit, drove him from his cabinet. Lincoln's reputation for kindness is based upon a number of trivial incidents and on his knack of juggling with words and using rhetoric to cover his absurd and often times outrageous statements by a jingle of sentences. He repeatedly backed down before his cabinet and had little of the backbone of his successor, Andrew Johnson.

20. Is there any truth in the statement that the South seceded from the Union because it saw itself menaced with the loss of the rule which it had enjoyed from the beginning?

None whatever. The Southerners never ruled the Union in any real sense. They controlled the executive department, but this department was confined to giving directions to the foreign relations and to executing the laws made by Congress. And this body, the lawmaking — the real ruler — was managed by the North from the very start. With the aid of a few delinquent Southern votes, the North could always count upon a majority in Congress. The revenue was chiefly levied on the products of the South, and was mainly disbursed in the North. Never once did the South use the machinery of the Federal

Government to enrich herself at the expense of the North. The funding of the National debt, the assumption of the State debts, the bounties for shipping, tonnage duties, bounties for the fishermen, the restrictions on foreign trade, the National bank, the tariff, the pensions, land grants, internal improvement, etc., were all in interest of the North. And this one-sided development remains today exactly like it was of old. The South is still "the milk cow of the Union."

About the Author

Lyon Gardiner Tyler was born in Virginia on August 24, 1853, to President John Tyler and First Lady Julia Gardiner Tyler. He was Tyler's fourteenth and next to last child.

He attended the University of Virginia, graduating in 1875. He served as president of the College of William and Mary in Willamsburg, Virginia, from 1888 to 1919 and is given credit for reviving the college from the financial depths it had fallen to at the conclusion of the War for Southern Independence.

Tyler was considered a noted educator and historian and in 1909, the centennial of Abraham Lincoln's birth, he became enraged by an article in a magazine which referred to his father, the 10th president of the United States, "as a dwarf when compared to Lincoln's presidency."

From then on he became a very staunch anti-Lincolnite and a very pro-Confederate commentator. He was a prolific author and published numerous pamphlets and booklets, including this one, which should be read by every American.

Tyler was a member of the Virginia Historical Society for 52 years, 32 years as its vice president. He was the author of several books on Virginia history.

"In Dr. Tyler's exhaustive researches in his task of vindicating the character and policies of his illustrious father, he chanced upon many literary misrepresentations concerning the War Between the States, discovered the systematic distortion of history by lying propagandists. Thus started his long-continued, tireless zeal for historical truth. Finding that his father's principles and ideals, for which he had stood and toiled throughout his long political career, including his

administration as president of the United States, were being misrepresented, Dr. Tyler set himself to correct these distortions and to defend his father's principles, especially the consistency of his position regarding States' Rights. Thus he came to write extensively on Confederate history and political philosophy."*

He passed away on February 12, 1935, in Richmond, Virginia, and is buried in Hollywood Cemetery.

* *The Sage of Lions Den* by John E. Hobeika

www.ingramcontent.com/pod-product-compliance
Lightning Source LLC
Chambersburg PA
CBHW021454080526
44588CB00009B/843